The Liberty
of the
Children
of God

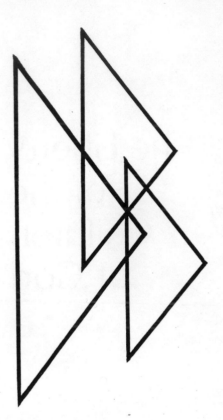

ALBA HOUSE
a division of
St. Paul Publications
Staten Island, N.Y.

The Liberty
of the
Children
of God

Bernard
Häring
C.SS.R.

Translated by Patrick O'Shaughnessy, O.S.B.

This book was first published by Verlag Winfried-Werk Gmbh., Augsburg under the title of *Der Christ und die Obrigkeit.*

Imprimi Potest:
    Bonaventure Knaebely, O.S.B.
Nihil Obstat:
    Daniel V. Flynn, J.C.D.
    Censor Librorum
Imprimatur:
    Terence J. Cooke, V.G.
New York, N.Y. — December 15, 1965
Library of Congress Catalog Number: 66-16472

Designed, printed and bound in the U.S.A. by the Pauline Fathers and Brothers of the Society of St. Paul at Staten Island, New York as a part of their communications apostolate.

CONTENTS

FOREWORD

The responsibility of Christians in the modern democratic state and the increased maturity of the laity so vitally necessary to the Church today force us to re-think the essence of authority and the corresponding question of obedience.

The conferences that I was permitted to hold concerning the "Relation of Christians to Ecclesiastical and Civil Officials" at the general meeting of Catholic women at Fulda, at the annual meeting of the men's society of the Diocese of Rottenburg and at the Catholic Education Society of Berlin met with such a lively response that, in view of their encouragement, I wish to make these thoughts available in an easily understandable and expanded form.

Bernard Häring, C.SS.R.

Introduction

"The Lord thy God made thee free."
(Deut. 15, 15)

INTRODUCTION

Not only the perfection of the individual personality but also the weal and woe of every human
society depend to a great extent on the correct
estimation of the true dignity and task of its rulers,
of their power and its limits. It is only on the
basis of correct understanding that the ruler will
know how to command correctly and that the subject
will find his right relation to authority. We shall
attempt to throw light on these important questions,
both for the sake of those in charge as well as for
the sake of those dependent on them. Most of us
have to fill both roles.

We shall first of all examine the basic religious
structure of the relationship of subject to ruler in
the light of the imitation of Christ. The most essential element to be considered here is the relationship
between Christ and the Father.

In the main section, therefore, we shall try to

determine the moral bases and presuppositions behind just ordinances and commands as well as those
which govern mature, Christian obedience.

Finally, we shall attempt to show how commanding and obeying both find their perfect expression
through the practice of the virtue of charity, the
law of Christ.

I

Looking to Christ and
the Father

"If the Son makes you free you will be free indeed."
(John 8, 36)

LOOKING TO CHRIST AND THE FATHER

IN THE LIGHT OF THE MOST SUBLIME MYSTERIES

Our relationship to authority in commanding and in obeying becomes truly Christian when we look to Christ and the Father with lively faith, for God is the source and the goal of all authority. God gives to earthly authority a share in his ruling power and fatherly love. In this giving there is reflected in various ways and depths the first and most profound of all the divine mysteries, that of the most holy Trinity, in which the Father, in and through the Holy Spirit, gives all that he has of power, glory and love to his Son, his co-eternal and co-equal Word. It is a mutual giving in which all three persons are forever involved. This mystery is made known to us through the Incarnation and anointing of Christ as king of all creation in and through the action of

the Holy Spirit. In him all authority has stability
and dignity. Our Lord said to his apostles, "As the
Father has sent me, so I send you." (John 20, 21)
This, the most sublime announcement in the history
of the world, places ecclesiastical authority expressly
in the ambient of the splendor of the highest of all
mysteries, of the procession of the Son from the
Father and of his being sent by the Father. The
Father sent the Son out of his infinite love so that,
through the kingdom of his love and grace, he might
announce to men the glory of his love. Human
authority should cooperate in this mission through
the power of the Holy Spirit and in a "spirit of
truth and love."

During his life on earth, our Lord joyfully announced to us that "all things had been given to
him by the Father." (Matt. 11, 27) Thus in him in
whom all things have been created, all earthly authority has its value. He, the Incarnate God, gives in a
mysterious way to the Church authorities a share
in his own service of love and in its splendor. If
the apostle, James, says to us, "There is but one
lawgiver and judge" (James 4, 12; see Isaiah 3,
22), and if Christ himself, speaking to the apostles
to whom he had given full power, gives them this

admonition, "But do not you be called 'Rabbi'...
for one only is your master, the Christ" (Matt. 23,
8ff), we still must not conclude that earthly authority
has been set aside or reduced to a sham. Rather
it has been elevated to a participation in the very
authority of creation's supreme lawgiver and Lord.
Therefore, all human authority looks for its model
to Christ and to his way of accomplishing the task
that he received from his heavenly Father.

GIFT OF GOD'S LOVE

Earthly authority is not only made resplendent by
the authority of the ruling God, but it also shares
in the love of the Good Shepherd, for God, the ruler,
is love. He has revealed his kingdom to be one
of love. His dominion, in fact, cannot be separated
from his love. He not only makes his authority valid
with infinite love, but his rule and his command
are the expressions of his entire being, of his love.
The basic condition for sharing intimately in this
dominion of love, both for rulers and subjects, is that
they serve God and neighbor in a spirit of love.

The great law of Christian life is grace, God's gift

of love. Basically we understand nothing of the law of God if we have before our eyes only or primarily his demands and the external tasks corresponding to them.

It is only when we understand God's gifts of love that we grasp what God really requires of us. In Christian teaching, laws and commandments are not complete or reserved categories; they are not something that have their end in themselves. What is Christian is essentially expressed primarily in grace, in love, in the gifts of God. The law and its moral-religious requirements are to be understood only as the other side of the coin of God's gifts. It is not the law that gives us access to the Good News, but it is the Good News of the love of God that gives us true access to the beauty and the pressing burden of the law of the New Covenant. Therefore, it is absolutely essential that we examine first of all the values that God bestows upon us by means of human authority.

If we wish to acquire an essentially Christian relationship to earthly authority, it is not enough to ask, "What shall we do when confronted by it?" The first question, without which we will get no complete and profound answer to the other, is this, "What part does God's love play in the exercise of human authority?" "What does God wish to say and give to us through it ... to us who are the subjects as well as the wielders of human authority?" By looking to God and to his loving intentions we will gradually enter into a more noble, joyful and thankful relationship with earthly authority. ~~By looking to God and to his loving intentions we will gradually enter into a more noble, joyful and thankful relationship with earthly authority.~~ Human authority has been given us by God in order that we might recognize in it a trace and a reflection of his dominion over all things. It is a created participation in his glory. Wherever it shows itself as genuine authority, and commands with equity, we must be taught by the Spirit of God to hear in it the voice of Christ who is the ultimate authoritative and all-embracing Word of the Father to us. All that he had to say to us, God manifested through Christ, his eternal Word. "He who hears you hears me; and he who rejects you, rejects me; and he who rejects me, rejects him who sent me." (Luke 10, 16) This was said to the apostles who were appointed by Christ to positions of authority in the religious affairs of the community. But in a general way all genuine authority stands under this law for all true authority touches in some way on this deepest mystery of the heart of God, namely, that the Father shares all things with the Son, and that the Son has made known to us the mysteries of his Father's heart. The master said to those who submitted themselves completely to his authority as beloved disciples: "No longer do I call you servants, because the servant does not know what his master does. But I have called you friends, because all things that I have heard from my Father I have made known to you." (John 15, 15)

A LOVING WORD AND ANSWER

Those who have earthly power are always in danger of the desire to bolster their authority by taking upon themselves grandiose titles and making their subjects feel the contrast as much as possible. By elevating themselves they hope to suppress their subjects. Christ used the fulness of his authority in a different way. As similar in many respects as his pedagogy may appear in comparison with that of other men, this one thing remains always ap-

parent: never does he manifest a desire to enslave
men or to reduce them to a state wherein they will
only feel his power. He is never seen trying to force
his will on men from without as a narrow-minded
"legalist" might.   On the contrary, he wishes to
receive us, over whom he has unlimited authority,
as his friends. In so far as he reveals to us the
inner mysteries of the holy Trinity, he shares with
us all that the love of God is, gives, and demands.
His authority makes friends out of his servants in so
far as he introduces them into the inner mystery
of the common life of the three Divine Persons and
from there shows them that they can correspond
completely to his loving authority only through
loving obedience.

All human authority, and most especially Church
authority, must be viewed in the light of this last
mystery because ecclesiastical authority is inserted
immediately into the supernatural mystery of God's
love and its first and proper task is to help us to
penetrate ever more deeply into the glories of this
divine love.   Civil authority also shares, in its own
way, in the dominion and love of God and, in so
far as it prompts us to esteem more highly the order
of God's creation, it serves us indirectly on our way

towards salvation. Its primary function is to create
a framework of order in which man can strive for
the coming of the kingdom of God and obtain salvation. Civil authority is not subservient to the
Church but, because it seeks above all else the
temporal common good, it does stand immediately
in the service of God. It is "God's minister to thee
for good." (Rom. 13, 4)

GOD'S GRACE

All authority is from God. It is given to parents
at the time when they first enter into natural relationship with their children. Through the holy sacra-
ment of matrimony, their authority is sanctioned
in a new way by the splendor of the authority of
Christ and his Church. The authority of the Church
was established by Christ in a solemn way. He
himself chose Peter, the twelve apostles, and the
seventy disciples, and sent them forth bearing the
fulness of his power. Did he also call an Alexander
VI by name into the sanctuary of the highest office
in the Church? Who would like to affirm that? Yet
when Alexander VI issued a command, he did it

by no authority than by that of the apostle Peter. But the authority of Peter and his successors was from Christ just as Christ in turn had received it from the Father. Therefore whoever obeyed the legitimate commands of an Alexander VI ultimately obeyed Christ and his heavenly Father. The authority of the state was established by God together with the creation of human nature, for considering the rapid growth of the human race, it was soon clearly apparent that family authority alone was not enough for the maintenance of social order. During his sojourn on earth Christ strengthened civil authority when he commanded that man "render unto Caesar the things that are Caesar's." (Matt. 22, 21) The apostle Paul, who on his missionary journeys experienced both the benefits of a stable state government as well as innumerable despotic encroachments and persecutions from rulers, says with emphasis that "there exists no authority except from God and those who exist have been appointed by God." (Rom. 13, 1) By that do we mean to teach a kingdom based on God's grace" and to reject as error the modern saying, "all power is from the people?" Yes and no! The authority of monarchs, no less than that of a democratic law-making corporation and government, is "based on God's grace." But neither Nero, Hitler, Stalin, nor Charlemagne, nor Louis the Pious were immediately chosen by God like David, any more than were the members of the legislatures and governments formed by them. In all these cases a part of the people, the elite, in a good or bad sense, bore the responsibility for the fact that precisely these men became the bearers of civil authority. And weren't the sins of the clergy and faithful, abstracting from the machinations of the Roman nobility, also guilty that an Alexander VI instead of a saint ascended the papal throne? Considering all the differences between an hereditary monarchy and a democratic state, or considering the great difference between the democratic election of a secular ruler and the handing over of Church power through the nomination and consecration of a bishop, it is very apparent that God does not choose the bearers of the governing power without making use of secondary causes. One might even say that generally not only do the people receive the government which they as responsible citizens deserve, but also that the Church of God receives the priests, bishops and Popes that it deserves, for it is the responsibility of all the faithful to pray, sacrifice and suffer for the vocation and consecration of the Church's leaders.

It would be too simple and false, however, to make the following distinction, namely, that the authority as such comes from God but the choosing of those who have the authority is the work of men. We must never overlook divine providence behind the secondary cause. This was clearly indicated to us when Christ said to Pilate, "You would have no power over me if it were not given to you from above." (John 19, 11) Here, too, looking to God is still the most important factor. In this light we see both our own responsibility to pray and co-operate in order that authority may be placed in the hands of those who are worthy, and at the same time our duty to recognize the rightful bearers of authority as ordained by God without consideration for their personal faults.

THE OBEDIENCE OF CHRIST

Our respect for earthly authority must be considered as an essential part of our following of Christ, for he himself, in the bosom of the Holy

Family, has given us a sublime example of humble obedience towards human authority, an example that was at the same time both genuine and mature.

When we speak of authority we do well to think of the family first. By seeing, in the relationship between authority and loving obedience as expressed in the life of the family, the prototype for the exercise of all human authority and obedience, we acquire access to the whole field in question. This is doubly important today in these times of unrealistic human relations in which society itself threatens the very existence of the individual personality. If authority does not find its roots within the family and if it does not reflect in some way and in all the areas under its domain a true family spirit it will necessarily sink into a heartless bureaucracy and sooner or later become inhuman. The child's first experience of authority in the form of loving, unselfish, solicitous parents is for it a necessary bridge to eventually entering into a genuine and personal, that is to say, into a trusting and understanding relationship with authority in general. A true sense of fatherliness and motherliness should be felt in all authority. Without it, genuine, democratic brotherhood is unthinkable.

For thirty years Christ by his example sanctified

obedience towards family authority. He also willing-
ly made himself subject to the spiritual authorities
in Judaism in so far as he, Lord and author of a
new spiritual order, could do so. He not only fulfilled the old law in the new, but he also obeyed it to
the extent that this was compatible with the new
law coming in his person. He obeyed the ritual and
civil laws of his people. Like every other Israelite of
twelve years of age, he made the pilgrimage to
Jerusalem. Regarding the authority of the Scribes
he said to his apostles, "All things that they command
you, observe and do." (Matt. 23, 3) By his example
he taught the same thing. But in virtue of the fulness
of power which belonged to him, he rejected their
usurpation of spiritual authority in order to make
their own additions into law. By his example he
also recognized secular authority when he commanded Peter to pay the taxes for them both.

Christ taught us, too, by his deeds that it is not
merely a perfect authority and one superior to us
that we must obey. He submitted himself as an
example to imperfect human authority when he took
up his abode in the sanctuary of the Holy Family.
Certainly he followed the guidance of a perfectly holy

mother and a holy foster father. But in regard to
holiness, wisdom and ability, he outdid them more
than any man can outdo his parents. He also submitted himself to the human limitation of their
knowledge which was a hindrance to them in spite
of their extraordinary holiness. Of the twelve-year
old Jesus, who through his wisdom, not only as-
tounded all the Jewish doctors, but also helped his
mother and foster father to an ever deeper understanding of his mystery when he asked them if they
"did not know that I must be about my Father's
business?" (Luke 3, 49) the Bible tells us that "He
went down with them and was subject to them."
(Luke 3, 51)

In his relationships with the Old Testament spiritual authority, Christ underwent his most bitter personal experiences of the weaknesses of human nature.
His beloved disciple once said of him that "he had
no need that anyone should bear witness concerning
man, for he himself knew what was in man," and he
said this not referring to Christ's divine but rather
to his human experiential knowledge.

But even though he knew, and knew painfully,
and had experienced as no one else ever had, how

even spiritual authorities can be obstinate, limited, and narrow-minded, he told his apostles that "he who hears you hears me." He knew the kind of man Peter was and yet he gave to him his full power of binding and loosing.

HUMBLE OBEDIENCE

To this correct Christ-like relationship with authority belongs the matter-of-fact awareness that those who have the power of ruling are imperfect men and that they have their limits, that even in some circumstances they can be notorious sinners. Our Lord and Master wanted to serve us in self-forgetting love. He became humbly obedient, not only to his most holy mother, but also to men who had to acknowledge themselves as grievous sinners. He revealed to us the riches of his love precisely in this extreme obedience, in "obedience to the death on the cross." It is incumbent upon us, therefore, as sincere followers of Christ that we do not limit our obedience to the direct commands coming from God but that we be ready to accept the will of God from the hands of others besides good, holy men. It is

not for us, as disciples of Christ, to demand that
the possessors of authority be a hundred percent
ideal, even though it is our right and to some extent
our sacred duty to be solicitous that the most capable
and most noble men be placed in the highest positions.   In principle we must be ready to accept
legitimate authority as it is, with its human limitations, and thus, in giving our obedience, we must be
ready for similar experiences as those that Christ
bore before us and for us.

TRUSTFUL YET CRITICAL OBEDIENCE

Christ obeyed human authority out of love for his
Father, but also with critical vigilance over the mis-
use of the power that had been given men from above.
He said to Pilate, "You would have no power over me
were it not given you from above." (John 19, 11)
The very moment in which the bearer of a power
not his own abused this power, Christ referred to
the authority of Almighty God.   His view penetrates
to the permission of the heavenly Father.   His loving
glance reaches to the last and most secret intention
of God's love.   Only true, deeply-rooted love—a love

that preserves trust above all things—is fully per-
ceptive. God does all things well. His doing is
always loving, because he is love itself. God acts
wisely when he loans authority to narrow-minded,
limited, yes, often to sinful men. Loving trust in
God's arrangements, even when through human
abuse, they bring suffering, is the distinguishing mark
of a Christian's attitude towards authority. Christ
shows us how this basic trust and loving assent
to Providence can be thoroughly bound up with a
clear judgment on man's abuse of power. Christ
shows Pilate his sin and refers to the greater sin
of the spiritual authority who had handed him over
to this unjust judge. "He who has betrayed me to
thee has the greater sin." (John 19, 11)

When our divine Lord and Master speaks to us
we know that he has the words of eternal life; he is
wisdom and goodness incarnate; he is the fulness of
all understanding. We do not always have that
same impression from human authority. On the
contrary, we are often very much aware that those
who have power are not very wise, perhaps also
not very kind or understanding to our needs. And
yet in a Christian and truly human way we can
only obey with great trust. But this trust that

THE MORAL FUNCTION OF AUTHORITY
AND OBEDIENCE

Human authority which shares in God's dominion and fatherly love, should never appear as a cold, impersonal, juridical machine or as a powerful person backed by force of arms and threat of punishment. A Christian will never equate morality with custom or the ordinances of human superiors. But he, society, and the superior must always be concerned with viewing their acts in the light of the latest moral teaching. The relationship of the Christian to authority must be thoroughly moral. This demands that the exercise of authority and the practice of obedience be guided and sustained 1) by the sanctity of one's moral standards, 2) by the strength of one's moral freedom, and 3) by the maturity and depth of one's moral conscience.

AUTHORITY AND MORAL KNOWLEDGE

Guidance, obedience and responsibility borne in common must stem from high moral standards, that is, from a correct understanding of moral principles and their application to concrete cases. To see this clearly we must first of all consider the various kinds and degrees of moral knowledge. This knowledge can increase and progress from a lifeless, rote-memory type of understanding of the law to a clear evaluation of it, then to a powerful penetrating feeling of its value, and finally to the most intimate kind of appreciation of the good which proceeds from one's interior personal relationship with it.

a. Knowledge of the law and trust in its worth

The lowest degree of moral knowledge is a barren, lifeless understanding of the law that tells us what is commanded and what is forbidden. We know the formulas, the letters and the immediate sense of the letter. This is a deplorable stage if it does not go further, especially in view of the law of the New Testament which springs from a sense of the inexhaustibly deep value of love's most splendid mysteries. And yet a knowledge of the law that is not very lively can be an important beginning. The knowledge of the law becomes truly moral when behind it there stands trust, more or less grasped in its entirety, namely that what is demanded here and now, what should be, is in itself good, or that the one who commands is good, therefore his command will be good also.

Knowledge of the law plays a great role in the life of a young child, although we by no means wish to deny him its deeper moral sense. The child who has just reached the use of reason cannot recognize immediately the meaning behind the thing commanded. Are not the parents glad when the child rightly comprehends what is demanded of it? This grasp of a command becomes true moral knowledge only if it does not remain an empty, fruitless understanding of the law. Above all else the inner value of the thing commanded must shine forth. We may not expect from a child an immediate evaluation from its own knowledge of the reason why the thing commanded is good. But we may expect a very meaningful trust: "That which is asked of me cannot be otherwise than good! Why?

Because my father and my mother are good. They can only will good for me and from me." A great crisis will begin once this genuine childlike trust is shaken before the child is able to penetrate to the proper sense of the command, to the genuine source of the good behind it. This crisis will be occasioned not only by carelessness on the part of those who are rearing the child, but can also be brought on by apparently unreasonable contradictions between one command and another or more importantly through contradictions between the commands of one parent and those of the other. When the child finally knows what "he has to do," it no longer knows if what it has to do is the good.

This simple knowledge of the law is very imperfect if it is at the same time morally doubtful; it does however play an important role in the process of moral development towards an ever more perfect type of moral knowledge, if behind it there stands a well-grounded and ever increasing trust in the individual who is giving the commands as a moral authority, the law as a moral power, and the possessor of the ruling power as a morally good person, and finally in the goodness of God who guarantees the value of one's obedience.

b. Personal evaluation

Our knowledge of the law should be increased
by a personal lively evaluation of it so that we recognize duty ever more clearly as the language of
value, as the language of the love of the one who
commands, manifesting itself in a well-understood
invitation to do something good, for only the true
good can be the basis of an obligation. But the
good is ultimately that which proceeds from true
love and corresponds to a love of the good. A full
moral recognition consists in this, that we, in the
task assigned us, hear the language of love, that is,
that we first see the splendor of the value inherent
in the obligation. This moral recognition, which
deduces the presence of an obligation from the value
inherent in a command or clearly surmises behind
the obligation the value that gives it validity, has
again several different degrees: from a penetrating
intellectual grasp of the value, to a spiritual feeling
regarding it, and finally to an immediate perception
and lively response of the whole person to it. The
highest degree in such an evaluation is a knowledge
of the law in the Johannine sense of the word

"knowing." To St. John "knowledge" does not consist merely in a momentary enthusiasm for the good,
but it arises rather from a profoundly intimate relationship between the one who thus knows with the
thing known, a permanent relationship of love for
the good. This knowledge is something entirely
special with regard to God for it is the beginning
of that "vision" of God already on this earth which
is granted by him to those who are "clean of heart."
(Matt. 5, 8) He who "knows God" in this sense
hears the word of God in the authority established
by him. (1 John 4, 6) " He who says that he knows
God and does not keep his commandments is a liar."
(1 John 2, 4) This knowledge comes ultimately
from an "anointing" by the Holy Spirit (1 John 2,
20); it is an outflowing from divine love, that is,
a sharing in the love of God itself. The knowledge
of God which proceeds from great love corresponds
to that true moral evaluation which, because it
springs from a sincere love for the good, does not
first demand that one be good, but presupposes that
he is. This inner knowledge and tasting of the good
is only possible when one is intimately united with
God, the source of all good, and when his love for
moral goods ultimately stands for his love of God.

c. Understanding the law in the form of love

Here below man is always developing. In the beginning his moral knowledge is far from perfect. It awakens slowly and must be deepened and clarified gradually. Superiors must give to the morally immature, the morally degenerate and above all children who are moral beginners, that knowledge of the law which will be necessary for their further development. They should present morality as an expression of love, in so far as they themselves command lovingly. By their being worthy of their charge, they will make it felt that trust in the goodness of the command is justified because the one who commands is good.

Authority must create the necessary framework for order if the standards of moral conduct in a community are to be raised. It must erect a bulwark for the law so as to prevent a "blind" obedience to it that might disintegrate into chaos because of ignorance or misunderstanding in its regard. The command that is merely understood externally *may* carry with it the possibility of later access to a knowledge of the inner beauty of one's duty, but it is only a starting point.

It must be clearly understood that laws, commands and warnings—even when they are morally understood—by no means exhaust the values of moral goodness. Moral knowledge must undergo continual progress regarding the relationships of justice with moral declarations involved in simple obedience to men. There exists for many the danger of seeing in human laws and their observance a full expression of the good. This danger must be lessened by the proper exercise of one's ruling power as far as possible.

Not even divine commandments can exhaust the inner riches of the goods made possible to us through grace. There are indeed, in the inexhaustible words of divine wisdom, express commands concerning our goal in life. Take for example the Sermon on the Mount or the chief commandment of love which express the full dazzling heights to which Christian morality can reach. But this will reveal itself to us only gradually in the course of a long process of maturing. Even the saint is never finished. He will always discover new sublime and valuable goals for which to aim. Besides the commands concerning our goal in life there are divine laws which have been formulated like human laws, for example the

Ten Commandments and the numerous admonitions contained in the New Testament. These are not the full expression of Christian perfection. Rather they are only warning signs and barricades. There is, however, a great temptation at times to take the warning signs for the law of the New Covenant itself, a temptation into which men in their exercise of human authority must not fall.

d. Stuck with the purely juridical

The laws and commands of human superiors present an ever greater danger to morality if they are made in such a way that the subject is content to do only that which is prescribed and thinks that by so doing he is perfectly good. It appears to me that for modern man there is a much greater danger in "blind" obedience to human laws, earthly dictates and decrees than there is in misunderstanding the New Testament and New Testament morality by giving it a juridic sense. Lutheran theology pictured the whole danger to morality as lying in a juridical understanding of the Gospel and thus it was often typified as a Christian sect that was inimical to law. So it was that to stem the tide of juridical anarchy the political sense of the law was emphasized more and more. Man was taught that he could and must observe the civil laws, even if he could not find in the Gospels and the warnings of Sacred Scripture any law or rule of faith for it or similar cases. Thus the warnings of the Gospel lost their inviolable validity in the conscience of many, while the dictates of men and the commands of human superiors became proper rules of moral activity (which, by the way, was not at all the purpose of the reformers concerning the political sense of the law). There are likewise many nominal Catholics for whom the danger of any kind of juridical approach to the Gospel scarcely exists, because they only know the civil sense of the law and restrict their contact with it to heeding the ordinances of other men. How often do you hear from lax Catholics, "I don't need to go to confession; I'm in good standing with God even though I don't go to Church; I haven't any sins for I was never in jail; I haven't stolen or killed anyone," etc. If some kind of punishment has not been incurred for the violation of the penal code or any attempt been made to disregard human authority, it is thought that this suffices.

There exists in the world today a frightening kind of existentialism, absolutely inimical to law of any kind, which trys to undermine the authority behind even the most essential of commands; an unhealthy form of situation-ethics which would sacrifice the law, which was established by God to draw man to God, not only to a falsely understood spirit of the times, but which also wishes to bend the law itself to the will of a world aligned against God (St. Paul would say: aligned in the direction of "the works of the flesh"). Moreover there are even among our average Christians, a great number of such "juridically"-minded men. What is not commanded them in juridical form or under threat of punishment, does not exist for them. What is not written out in capital letters, does not touch them. The "juridicist" has no access to enlightening moral values. For him, such values have no splendor because he has too little love within his heart, because he has not become, through love, a man who truly sees. It is the task of parents and of those caring for souls to educate them to a recognition of the good out of love for it. They, before God, must try to elevate their charges above that level of moral conduct in which they do only what is commanded by human superiors to a discovery of the infinite riches of the good behind these commands. Education to obedience demands not only that one bring to light the inner value of obedience as such, but, wherever it is possible, also the moral value of that which is commanded.

Even as far as the Church, which is the bride of the Holy Spirit, is concerned there is the danger that one may allow himself to be guided solely by its precepts. A person knows that the Church demands this particular thing. Therefore he does it without thinking of the reason or purpose behind the law or command and then feels that he can consider himself a good Christian. This is only possible because he has not yet learned that the original and fundamental law of the Church and of every individual Christian is "the spiritual law of life in Christ Jesus" (Rom. 8, 2). The Spirit of God does not command arbitrarily for God is the Spirit of truth. One should seek to understand the laws and commandments of the Church authorities and should try to uncover

in them the deep and final purposes of the Holy
Spirit, always of course with humility for we cannot
penetrate to the thoughts of God, and when he reveals
them to us we can never fully grasp them.   Our
obedience can be a lively and enthusiastic obedience
only when we open ourselves to the "Spirit of truth,"
and so try to understand and to fulfill the inner
sense of that which is given to us by the bride of
the Holy Spirit.

If nothing else, the painful experiences of the
limitations inherent in all human authority should
awaken those who obey without thinking and force
them to take a second look and not to view external
laws and commands as though there were nothing
else.   We shall never arrive at a truly animated
knowledge of the law, if the effort concerning moral
knowledge is concentrated on the law or on human
dictates and commands and nothing more.   Superiors, including Church superiors, must do their best
so that the subject is not left hanging to the letter
of the law which is something external, but that he
come to an inner vision of the good, both that demanded by the law and that which lies outside the
law.

e. No criticism vs. uncharitable criticism

It is only out of a moral knowledge which takes us beyond the mere explanation of law and right that there can grow a genuine power to distinguish rightly. Those, superiors included, who cannot discern spirits and evaluate them correctly forfeit the obedience of men. Whoever does not take the trouble to uncover the true golden basis of Church and civil law will never be able to distinguish the gold from the tinsel and will fall into a superficial service of the letter of the law. The more meaningful the content of a law and the more reasonable a superior's admonition, so much the more apt is it that, lacking a living spirit, the letter of the law will "kill." (cf. Cor. 3, 6) To remain bogged down in a simple knowledge of the law carries with it the danger of a dull lack of criticism or of a criticism proferred without love; both manifest a lack of moral insight and of genuine moral effort.

Lack of criticism is indeed an indication of subordination, but it could never be considered a true and dignified kind of Christian obedience. One who never criticizes, whether he realizes it or not, is actually guilty of foolishness and lust for power.

He is a stone with which dictators build their streets.
If he is fortunate, he will get a good superior, but
he will never be able to enter fully into the real
moral and religious aims of the superior. Who knows
whether or not the one who is afraid to criticize,
who today follows the ruler without any problem,
may perhaps tomorrow, thoughtlessly and without
misgiving, obey the unenlightened words of the
spirit of the world?

Criticism without love proceeds from unenlightened zeal. The grumbler does not exercise love
or dedication to the welfare of the community. He
cannot distinguish between person and thing. He
sprinkles his venom on the office as well as upon
the one who holds the office. He not only scourges
the human weaknesses of the office-holder, but without noticing it, he tears down his authority as well.
Charitable criticism, and this alone, is worthy of a
Christian for it alone proceeds solely from a deep
insight into the splendor of the good and from a
true evaluation of it which awakens all man's powers
of love.

The superior who seeks to cultivate in the immature a mere undecerning obedience, because he
thinks thus to attain his goal more easily, either

smoothes the way for the slave-keeper of tomorrow
or reaps loveless criticism.

It is dangerous to initiate a child too soon to
criticism. For the child there should be a natural
trust in adults until he has gradually learned to
understand why the parents give this command rather than another. They should be gradually taught
to distinguish clearly between the authority which
parents have from God, their good intentions, and
the unavoidable imperfection in their exercise of
authority. If educators wish to prevent the child
from becoming critical towards them and their authority, they must start early to develop in the
child its ability to distinguish the true and to criticize
the false charitably. It is not without reason that
God has given the child such a strong inclination for
asking questions. At first the child asks superficially,
then it goes deeper and deeper in wanting to know
the why of everything. If the parents impatiently
answer: "What does it matter to you? It should be
enough for you that we say so," the child will gradually become critical of the father and mother and
will acquire a feeling of mistrust: "Why don't they
tell me? Perhaps they don't know themselves, or
perhaps they don't care for me." Here we may see

the beginning of a dangerous kind of criticism or perhaps of a later sickly mania for criticizing. If however the parents give an amiable explanation, suitable to the child's comprehension, and encourage the child to investigate things thoroughly, the child will not immediately understand everything, but it will become firmer in its obedience because its obedience will be based on trust: "It is right because father and mother say so; they know what they're talking about." This trust will become enlightened and more firmly based according to the measure in which the capacity for distinguishing is developed. It will keep the child from falling into habits of malicious criticism when it makes the discovery that the intelligence and moral perfection of its parents have perceptible limits. The healthily developing critical sense (here understood in the literal sense as a discerning understanding) then takes on moral relevance without at the same time undermining all authority.

The same thing holds in regard to Church authority which should lead Christians to the fullness of age in Christ, to true Christian maturity. (Eph. 4, 13) The establishment of the Apostles as shepherds of the Church along with the parable of the good shepherd point up the solidarity that must exist between the shepherd and the flock. Authority must not be enforced with staff and dog—must never cause the suspicion of arbitrariness. That would be the case, for example, when a pastor wished to arrogate all to his own will, instead of lovingly and understandingly explaining to those under him the reason behind his commands. If one is introduced to the reasons for obedience as well as to the significance behind individual Church laws, by means of a considerate explanation of the same instead of through mere legalistic casuistry, he will acquire over and above the mere knowledge of the law, a heart and will corresponding to his evaluation of it. Thus the Christian will be led, also in regard to Church authority, to discern correctly and perhaps then and there he will form his own conclusions; but precisely the development of one's powers of discernment will stem the tide of a loveless refusal to criticize as well as an uncontrolled mania for criticism.

As far as all the commandments of the Church are concerned, beginning with the precepts of fasting, of abstinence, of the Eucharistic fast, to the much more difficult laws regarding marriage, divorce, etc., the moral and religious values which apply here must come from within if they are to be truly enlightening. Of course one cannot do away with the difference between Church laws determined by historical circumstances, the divine laws which the Church has surrounded or protected with other laws of her own, and finally, the unchangeable laws that God has given along with nature or with the very essence of the Church. The formulation of its laws as well as the mentality itself in Church circles was partly dependent on the spirit of positive law which received its validity from the arbitrary will of the state alone. The Church never denied the existence of certain fundamental laws which supported all the others, but it did, in the course of time, follow the lead of positive law and establish a large number of prescriptions of a juridical nature. Catholic moral teaching was never intended to imitate the spirit of the Talmud, which places a thousand and more individual legal prescriptions on the same moral level. A very poor service would be done to Canon Law, which lays down the individual laws of the Church, if one would try, through a false explanation of their sense, to dogmatize laws made to cover specific cases at specific times in the history of the Church. In this way Canon Law would soon lose all its adaptability. But to make references to those conditions which called for the passage of a law in the first place—conditions whose disappearance may later make the law superfluous—is to give an adequate explanation of the sense of the law. Such an explanation is more consonant with the pastoral care of the Church, with God's great commandment of love, and with that love which is vigilant for the present needs of those in its care.

When the Christian is taught lovingly and perseveringly to distinguish between the unchangeable laws which proceed immediately from the hand of Almighty God, and the historically conditioned expression of the pastoral love of the Church, obedience may perhaps for a time be more painful, but it will at the same time become more "moral" and sublime because it will be based on a genuine moral evaluation of the will of God in each individual case. The power of distinguishing thus developed may perhaps necessitate reform, not always a pleasant thing, among the Church authorities, but it will in the long run save them from loveless criticism and a total disregard of their authority.

OBEDIENCE IN TRUE LIBERTY

The first moral bond between superiors and subjects is based on their appreciation of the same moral
values.   The second equally important root of a
moral union between superiors and subjects is moral
liberty, which should develop more and more into
the full liberty of the children of God.   Human
authority itself and obedience to it should be the
shortest route to achieving this sort of liberty.

a. False ideal of liberty and the liberty of the children of God

What is liberty?   The Christian's idea of liberty
is entirely different from that of anarchists, liberals
and Marxists.

The anarchist sees in any order the greatest im-
pediment to his liberty.   His goal is unlimited freedom for his unbridled instincts and passions.

The liberal sees the danger to liberty in a truth
that binds all.   Therefore he fights against the teaching authority of the Catholic Church and against
the denominational school, which is built upon a

clear confession to an obliging truth, enlightening the entire field of one's life. The liberal wants to be free *from*, not free *for* an absolute or free *for* valid ideals such as are included in the Christian concept of truth and justice. As in the field of commerce he praises the liberty of the strong, so in the cultural and secular philosophical fields he esteems above all the liberty of a few "strong spirits."

The Marxist sees liberty in an absolute emancipation from ethical and religious ideals, which he regards as an ideological means of gaining power for the governing class. He thinks he will become free through the insights of "scientific socialism" in the natural process of history's course in dialectic tensions, in class war and class hatred. For him liberty means an increase in the legislation governing the processes of social production according to principles layed down by Marx, Lenin and Stalin.

For the modern heathen existentialist liberty presupposes the denial of all moral norms and of all laws. He feels free only when his action has no other goal than the demonstration of his own freedom. He wishes to feel his power, not only to give his actions ever new forms nowhere seen before, but also to impress on himself, through his own invention, a way of being a man never thought of until now, but not as a firm and permanent form.

In view of the many contradicting ideas of liberty, the Christian today must know what *he* understands by the term. For the Christian, moral liberty is the inner power of the will to put itself to the service of the good from the strength derived from its own insight and evaluation of the good. The Christian sees in his liberty a created sharing in the liberty of God which is not a blind force and impulse, but truth and love. God the Father is the self-knowing one who gives all his riches to his Word and this, his Word, "is not just any word but *the* Word that (together with the Father) breathes forth love, the Holy Spirit." "God is love." (1 John 4, 8 and 16). This phrase means at the same time that "God is light; in him there is no darkness" (1 John 1, 5). All that God does outside himself he does "in the Word" (1 John 1, 3) in clear visible love. In God there is no coercion, no lack of liberty, because all is enlightened by his truth. His love is a reflection of the truth; his activity, nothing but love.

Man becomes free in the measure that he becomes more like God. He grows through the grace of God to the glorious liberty of the children of God when he is not pushed by force or fear, but loves the good from inner conviction, and fulfills it out of love. The liberty of the children of God reaches its highest degree when it allows itself to be led entirely by the Spirit of God. "The Lord is spirit. But where the spirit of the Lord is, there is freedom" (2 Cor. 3, 17). The liberty of the children of God presupposes that one hold oneself free from the impotence of sin and the slavery of Satan, that out of inner free choice one submit to the law of Christ and that he in no way hide behind the written law. Thus the Christian holds himself open in a true spirit of freedom to the will of God manifesting itself at every hour through the pull of grace and in the call of changing situations. Since the liberty of the children of God is a gift from God the Christian knows that he can receive it, keep it and increase it only through unconditioned docility and pliancy to the will of his only teacher and master, Christ, who enlightens us both from within through his "Spirit of truth" and from without in his word, his example, his Church and every legitimate superior.

b. Education to inner liberty

With this understanding of moral liberty and the liberty of the children of God, the moral function of superiors and of obedience to them must be considered.

No human authority can take away from us that intimate struggle for personal freedom of which only the seed has been given us, but it can support us therein. Authority must above all at times by using force, hold in check whatever is evil in man in order to protect the liberty of the good in him that it may be made manifest. Wickedness and thoughtlessness again and again have written the word LIBERTY in big letters on their banners in order to eventually strangle the true liberty of the good or to make it impossible for them to use it. On the other hand those in authority must possess a reasonable amount of power to enforce their legislation. Authority often enough has to protect the morally unprepared against the arbitrariness of their own wicked designs; it must protect them from that moral disorder in society in which man's inner liberty would suffer its greatest injury. The immature person must be strictly held

to a minimum of legislation if genuine liberty is
ever to grow and ripen within him. The outer framework of order, which superiors through their laws
and their art of educating must guarantee, is necessary in order that the fullness of the liberty of God's
children blossom forth in an atmosphere of love.

Superiors must strive from the beginning to see
to it that their commands give ample consideration
to the subject's inner freedom. This holds true for
all superiors who must deal with people, for civil
as well as ecclesiastical authorities, and above all
must it hold true in any democratic regime. A
superior must never make his the motto: "Oderint
dum metuant." Every state will sooner or later
become despotic and unworthy of the men it pre-
tends to serve if it ever ceases to be concerned about
whether or not its citizens follow its ordinances with
a true sense of interior liberty and moral responsibility. The principle that the exercise of one's interior liberty must be evoked by civil authority holds
in an incomparably higher way in all parental and
ecclesiastical guidance and education. Parents and
church superiors fail to attain their goal when they
are concerned only with external order and sub-
mission but not with the good use of the moral

liberty of their subjects. Moral goodness is affirmed
and fulfilled only when it is the expression of one's
interior liberty.

There are among parents, educators and cate-
chists, it is sad to say, too many tamers, masters of the
art of training, who are satisfied with themselves and
their subjects when they have achieved some kind
of external order by any method whatsoever. The
man who has great ruling power is always tempted
to becoming a tamer. His will must be done, order
must be maintained. He is more disturbed by small
disorders, by violations of his often meaningless rules,
than by his own sins which may not be small. In
that the tamer betrays himself, for instead of being
restless and having solicitude for the growth of the
moral liberty of those entrusted to his care, instead
of possessing a loving heart and enthusiasm for the
good that can only be attained through the exercise
of one's liberty, he expresses hurt and anger because
his will, the will of the superior, is not done.

The goal of parental and church authority is not
external conformity but the dominion of Christ over
hearts, a dominion of his life of grace and love. To
this, force and the preservation of external order offer
only an indirect contribution. Therefore moral per-

suasion, the winning of another's free will through one's own enthusiasm for the good must take first place. Also, good order in a community is something worthy of love. Rightly brought about, it can help a great deal to make one free, just as can law based on true understanding and love. Above all, however, a love, growing from firm convictions, for man's natural and supernatural common good should be awakened in the interests of the community.

Liberty increases to the extent that narrow-minded egoism is overcome. The inner power for good, flowing from high, courageous ideals, is perfected by an enthusiastic love of the good and a readiness to give oneself for God and neighbor. The permanent enlivening and deepening of moral motives stand above and beyond any external accustoming to order and to good. Reward and punishment can only be used as helping and supporting motives, gradually to be decreased as one grows in moral maturity. Praise and rebuke are to be used in such a way that they bring to the surface and enliven one's consciousness of the corresponding hidden values in one's free choice.

Christian liberty is a liberty of the children of God that essentially surpasses every juridical re-

lation. St. Paul made a great effort to defend this
liberty against the arbitrary repression of it or dis-
crimination against it by any juridical regime. "You
are not under the law but under grace" (Rom. 6,
14). That does not by any means imply that the
Christian does not have to obey any law, but that
the bouyancy of his liberty may not be destroyed
or tied down in his carrying out of juridical prescriptions. A man's service to the law and his subjection
to a superior must never become something inani-
mate but must take its place alongside his free moral
and religious life which proceeds immediately from
grace. All things have their proper place in the law
of man's newly reacquired freedom in Christ and his
law of grace and love, including his relationship
towards earthly authority. And this implies a strict
obligation on the part of authority as well as on the
part of those who obey.

c. Liberty under the law of grace

Because the liberty of the children of God is
guaranteed only by the law of grace, parents and
Church authorities must make every effort that the

exercise of their dictates resemble and be in agreement with that law. Human authorities must, resembling Christ, so command, that their precepts may be understood as a gift, as an expression of their care and love, yes, that it may be grasped as a sharing in the love of Christ itself. The subject must correspondingly strive to render his obedience as thanks, to offer it ultimately to Christ in a spirit that corresponds to the law of grace. The spirit of the liberty of God's children is not acquired or else it is discarded when, confronted by Church precepts, a Christian merely asks, "What must I do or omit in order not to break the law?" To illustrate the situation with an example that is well known, the question is often heard, "Do I fulfill the law if I am bodily present at Sunday Mass without making any earnest effort at inner devotion?" "Yes," is the answer often given, "it is enough, for the law cannot demand more than its physical fulfillment." If the Christian, however, determines to be merely present bodily at Mass, without disturbing anyone and behaving correctly, he shackles himself and is no longer free with the liberty that should be his as a child of God. He has placed upon his shoulders an intolerable yoke and a law which, because never properly evaluated, is unable to serve the cause of grace and true freedom. The Christian fulfills the law of the Church with the liberty of one of her children only when he interiorly enters into her purpose and the purpose of Christ through his comprehension of the meaning in his life of the holy sacrifice of the Mass. This infinitely sublime sacrifice of thanksgiving is the love-feast of God's people with Christ, their High Priest. Only he who recognizes behind every command the great gift which God makes of himself to mankind in them and strives from his knowledge of this great grace thankfully to fulfill outwardly and, more important still, inwardly what is offered to him in this manner, truly acts with the liberty of a child of God.

The inner riches and dynamism of the liberty of the children of God must far outdo the impulse created by that which is commanded by the letter of the law. The Christian must never become so awed by the barricades placed before him by the law that he no longer has enough strength and adaptability to raise the essential question, "What is God asking of me here and now? What is there in this command that corresponds to the present need of my neighbor and the requirements of God's

kingdom." Authorities must be careful not to strangle the life-giving strength of the interior liberty of
their subjects. The law of the New Testament, which
for a man devoid of love is simply unattainable, must
manifest itself, according to the words of St. Augustine, as "an easy law for those who love." This great
Father of the Church later sharply rebuked "those
who overburden even the worship of God (which in
his mercy God, through the celebration of but a
few understandable mysteries, wished to establish
as a religion of perfect liberty) with so many slavish
prescriptions, that in comparison with it, the position
of the Jews, who were subject only to the law of the
Old Testament and not to any arbitrary human additions, was more bearable." St. Thomas who freely
subjected himself to a rule that was not easy, cites
these words of St. Augustine, and with him warns of
a juridical accumulation of burdens imposed from
without (S.T.: I, II, q. 107, a. 4). No one will despise these great saints and theologians and accuse
them of not sufficiently recognizing authority or of
being guilty of laxity. They saw that the Christian,
placed under too many juridical demands, especially
if they are in any way arbitrary, is no longer in a
position to fulfill these prescriptions with a lively

sense of love. He soon ceases to preserve and increase his interior liberty. The law of grace, which cannot be juridically pin-pointed, loses its efficacy and the opportune call of God through the present situation and the inner urge of grace no longer makes itself heard.

If parents give a thousand orders and make a thousand prohibitions, commanding all day and grumbling about little things, how can the child be expected to learn to use its God-given liberty? It will never be able to acquire the maturity and balance so characteristic of the joyful liberty of the children of God. Rarely will its obedience rise above a perfunctory doing of that which is commanded from without. Because the parents, by reason of so much directing, will soon lose their capacity to make the child enthusiastic for the good, the child will grow up lacking the power of moral invention, the ability to contemplate in silence the urgings of the inner voice of his conscience and the desire to pay loving attention to the needs of his neighbor.

If the Church is making fewer and fewer laws, besides those that are immediately demanded by human nature and the order of grace, and if tomorrow it should decide to relax its precepts of fast

and abstinence, we must not come to the conclusion
that it is satisfied with a moral and religious minimum. On the contrary, it wishes to make us ever
freer and lead us on, through an inner renewal of
sacramental piety and a lively introduction into
Christ's sacrifice of love, to an asceticism that fits
our times, and to a reservoir ready for sacrifice for the
concerns of the kingdom of God. In her wisdom the
Church no longer sees the necessity in legislating
so narrowly in such areas as the forbidding of books,
of censuring films, etc., because it realizes that its
most important work consists in educating her children to the highest degree of responsibility possible,
to a joy-filled liberty which infinitely surpasses any
juridical limits. The Christian must know when he
goes beyond the mere demands of the external law.
The lawbreaker will never attain true liberty because he is always tearing down the barriers of the
law placed there to protect him from the slavery
of sin. He will never attain the liberty of the children of God who sees always and only the barricades
in front of him. How unfortunate the beast that,
in a pasture verdant and fine, chooses instead to
walk the fenceline and to eat the weeds and die.
How poor the Christian who has only been taught

to walk the line but has never been shown the glory of the riches of his liberty enclosed by it, the steep summits of true liberty and perfection.

The liberty of God's children does not consist in refraining from all that is difficult and great. It consists rather in preserving oneself free from the slavery implicit in the question, "Must I still do this or that juridical work?"

d. Liberty from arbitrariness and narrowness

This central problem of true freedom places stiff requirements on authority as well as subject. The prudent limiting of external laws is not enough. It all boils down to always looking to the end for which the law ultimately exists, to the love of God which directs and guides all things, not through the letter of the law alone, but through the charitable exercise of its spirit. St. Thomas teaches that that which is most proper in the law of the New Testament and that in which its whole power consists is the grace of the Holy Spirit. All that the New Testament contains as well as all the guidance of superiors through the Church and parents in caring for the souls of its children should "serve for the spreading of God's grace and for the right use of the grace of the Holy Spirit" (Summa Theol. I, 2; q. 106, a. 1). Both the possessor of authority as well as the subject must first see that they attach themselves more and more in their interior life to the guidance of the Holy Spirit and the loving purpose of God. That is what is meant when we say that both in the commanding as well as in the obeying the spirit of true liberty must dominate. Both must remain free from arbitrariness, lack of spirit and narrowness in their execution. The Christian must know that he has no right to speak of the liberty of God's children if he is not ready for an energetic fight against "the works of the flesh," pride and sloth, and as long as he still continues to cleave to the mere letter of the law.

From the State we cannot demand or expect a positive education of men to the liberty of God's children. Such an education pertains directly to the Church and to Christian parents. It is, however, true that in our relations with civil authorities a spirit corresponding to this liberty must prevail. A true democracy stands or falls depending on whether or not its citizens have been educated to a spirit of true, free, and joyful responsibility. According to its nature the State must work with force and external conformity with its laws more so than must the family and the Church. But when the State trusts only in external obedience of its precepts and the corresponding means it has of compelling such obedience, it is on the way to dictatorship. The State, like the Church, needs virtuous, free and responsible men for its proper development.

Traditional moral theology expresses this spirit of genuine liberty and courage to personal initiative on the part of its subjects by her use of the term *epikeia*. *Epikeia* enables one to interpret and to fulfill laws and commands more intelligently and more in a way corresponding to the situation than the letter is able to express. Some perhaps have at times made out of this noble virtue a kind of bed of roses which gave them the right to ask, "Must I do that also? How can I avoid that oppressive law?" Instead of sensing behind the letter of the law the presence of the Spirit, they were inclined to find there a reason for excusing and dispensing themselves from it entirely. The true spirit of liberty is not idle or lazy. It doesn't waste its energy on useless things, but it has the courage to look the demands of reality in the eye, to take the initiative when necessary and the responsibility when it would be more comfortable to withdraw. *Epikeia,* the virtue of the Christian concept of liberty, presupposes genuine readiness for obedience, readiness for the call of God through the needs of the hour, the gift of distinguishing, mature prudence which proceeds only from love, from a warm, vigilant interest in oneself and the community. For that, experience, schooling and above all, an authority animated with the spirit of Christian liberty, that is, with true docility to the Spirit of God and permanent readiness for the call of the hour, are needed.

CONSCIENTIOUS OBEDIENCE

When those who possess authority are filled with a lively capacity for making accurate evaluations and when they possess as well a true spirit of liberty and strive to inculcate these gifts into those entrusted to their care, then only can they reasonably expect the blossoming forth of a relationship based on an obedience that is at once Godlike and sincere.

Obedience does not imply in the first place a relationship of obedience to men, but rather one of union with God through one's own conscience. Commanding and obeying must be exercised in a spirit of obedience that in the last analysis subordinates all to God. A moral and religiously developed conscience places all its activity in the hands of God.

Obedience requires of those giving orders an earnest examination of conscience: "Am I commanding only that which I in conscience feel to be the will of God in this case? Am I obeying God when I command?" In conscience one must not only look at obedience as something given to men but must consider it as something offered to God.

Human authority can command morally only in so far as it obliges in conscience. When it only imposes an external burden, but cares little about obliging in conscience, the exercise of the power of authority is not in a full sense moral; it remains more or less on the plane of taming or training. Conscience and authority are interrelated. Where a subject's conscience is not vigilant, the command of authority finds no moral echo. Conscience however needs guidance in many ways; it needs to be protected by authority, to be developed and led by it. Without authority man's conscience would not reach maturity. Just as a dignified social life can

never be formed without authority and law, so too
is it with the development of a mature conscience.

Since the Church and civil authorities do not in
every way have the same functions with regard to
the conscience of their subjects, the two roles must
be considered separately, although what is said in
regard to Church authority partly—indeed only partly—holds true also of the other authority and vice
versa.

a. Conscience and Church authority

The conscience of the faithful receives from the
teaching authority of the Church, as something very
precious, an infallible security in basic moral truths.
When the infallibility of the Pope was defined and
Cardinal Newman was asked, "What about the teaching of your own conscience?" he gave a classic Catholic answer in so far as he extolled first conscience and
then the infallibility of the Pope. He retained his
high estimation of conscience in the statement, "I
have always affirmed that obedience to conscience,
even to an erring conscience, is the best way to the
light" (Apol., Ch. 5). Conscience is the guiding star

that we must follow always and in every circumstance. But how negligent I would be in my conscience if I never attain any certain knowledge about good in things that are basic! The more certain our moral knowledge is, and the more splendidly the truth concerning moral good is announced to us so much the more urgently will our conscience be able to urge us to do this good. If I do not know what God's will is, if in my conscience I am confused about basic truths and do not know what God teaches me and demands of me, I can no longer render any conscientious obedience but must limit myself to a further search for the truth. That is precisely the task of the Church in regard to the conscience that is really seeking the truth. It is the Church's duty to place before the eyes of her children God's law of love unfalsified, and to point out to them the requirements of this love and grace. If it can infallibly and in all its essentials place this before them, it will have, at least in all critical matters, served their consciences well.

Conscience needs authority to safeguard her in the truth; faith and obedience in their turn require conscience if they are to be morally fruitful. The Christian conscience and Church authority are intimately bound up with one another. What the Holy Spirit teaches us through the Church, he also teaches us through conscience. He is the one Spirit who in and through the Church works in us and manifests to us the law of grace. He is the Spirit of the eternal God, the Spirit of truth and of love who enlivens our conscience from within and awakens in us the power of love that urges us on to good. Therefore St. Paul speaks of "my conscience bearing me witness in the Holy Spirit" (Rom. 9, 1). Christ indicates a deep mystery when he names the Holy Spirit the "Spirit of truth" (John 14, 17). "He will teach you all the truth. For he will not speak on his own authority, but whatever he will hear he will speak—he will receive of what is mine and declare it to you." The Holy Spirit is entirely personal, the personal gift of love. As the personal love of the Father and Son, he teaches us all truths as seen in the light of this love and gives us proper access to them, for the deepest knowledge of truth can come only through love. And "God is love" (1 John 4, 8).

Through the Holy Spirit who is poured out upon her, the Church is a community of love and the guardian of truth. The carrying out of her teaching and pastoral office, all her valid commands are basically an expression of love. As the Church teaches and leads in a spirit of love so the Christian understands her truth and her laws in a salutary way only when his conscious obedience is full of a sincere and intimate docility towards the Holy Spirit. The "Spirit of truth" is the love of God working in us and in the Church. The relationship between Church authority and the faithful subject to it becomes perfect and truly representative of the spirit of the New Testament only when both at all times hear the voice of God in their conscience and when they are docile to the Holy Spirit making known the truth to them through love.

Regarding the infallible teaching of the Church in matters of faith and morals there is no tension between Church authority and a genuine Christian conscience; for in this case the Christian is absolutely certain that those in authority are completely docile to the "Spirit of truth." Hence it is significant that the conscience of the mature Christian know the limits within which the Church teaches us with infallible certainty. Besides this, it must know that there is a wider field in which the Church leads and commands authoritatively but not infallibly. Here it may happen that the subject refuses the light of

the Holy Spirit, or because of some human defect
is innocently blinded to his truth. It may be, too,
that the one giving the command listens too little
to the Holy Spirit, or that he lacks the necessary insight or prudence, and the result will be a painful
conflict. Experience confirms the basic principle
which holds true here as well, namely, that Church
authorities usually and on the average enjoy greater
guidance from the Holy Spirit than the individual.

Regarding authority, precisely in cases of conflict,
the Christian must proceed from a thoroughly prudent "work hypothesis." Superiors understand things
better than I and they command more prudently and
unselfishly. Also in the field where the Church
teaches and guides in a way that is not infallible the
presumption of truth and right is in favor of her
authority. It is mere pride to presume that the law
is in the subject's favor or that the subject sees and
understands everything better than his superiors. In
humility the subject must be ready to obey, and
indeed in case of necessity, he must do so without
questioning. Humility, however, does not excuse
and free the Christian from making a choice, or
from sincerely sifting and judging facts and circumstances. When in doubt about the legitimacy of a

command the subject must in humility conclude that
God has given us a great aid to our conscience in
having established Church authority which he up-
holds through his Holy Spirit.   Until there is proof
of the contrary, the superior must be considered
good and prudent.

But when the subject, after serious examination
of conscience, and after examining the unselfishness
of his motives, and being conscious of the limitations
of his own view, has come to the conclusion that here
his conscience commands him to do otherwise, he
must follow his conscience no matter how painful
the results may be.   He may not carry out a command of a superior that is against his conscience.   But
his conscience is right only when he starts from the
correct point of view and does not ascribe to himself a kind of infallibility or consider Church authority as always laboring under great possibility of error.
One must have strong cogent reasons in conscience
to form such a judgment as, "Here the Church commands me unjustly; here the superior is in error; here
they are even demanding sinful things of me."

It is a sign of genuine conscientiousness when
both the one commanding and the one obeying are
aware of their limits.   All this holds as well for

Church authority wherever it is not a matter of infallible teaching, but concerns only the application of a general truth to the changing conditions of our times. Also the one who commands must have a gentle, humble mistrust of himself as to whether he is entirely led by the Spirit of God. He must ask himself again and again, "Do I in commanding practice vigilant obedience towards the Holy Spirit? Am I supernaturally prudent and do I have the necessary treasure of natural prudence to find the right thing?" There should be a piece of genuine humor bound up with the knowledge that "I, too, can be mistaken." A superior who is kind and has a sense of humor will not at once accuse others of lack of interest, love or obedience if they should happen to question some of his orders.

Church authority must consider one more thing. It is accustomed to speak in general terms. It is a traditional, preserving and very conservative power. It must be filled out, interpreted and corrected by men who, in daily life, experience its rough spots and the need of applying it to changing circumstances. In relation to the concrete situation and the change of conditions, superiors must be able to listen to and seek the constructive criticism of men and women who stand in the front lines of God's kingdom.

This was one of the great concerns of Pius XI. He wished that a responsible laity in Catholic action would not only be the organs for carrying out the orders of the hierarchy and clergy, but also that they might stand at the side of these same bishops and priests advising as well as supporting them. Much has been done in this direction since then. In Germany, for instance, leading Catholic men and women have been called to important priest conferences by the Ordinary. Their criticism and encouragement was not only given attention but also thanks and applause.

It is a common and ancient Christian practice for high Church authorities, in important questions concerning the care of souls, to seek the advice of leading lay persons and especially of Catholic organizations. Through it the position of authority in the Church is by no means weakened. Rather authority thus finds a more perfect way of commanding and assures itself of a stronger resonance.

Christian lay persons are not wanting today who are capable and ready to offer humbly and courageously their constructive criticism in earnest counsel and personal talks. Precisely through the seriousness with which the burning questions which affect the Church today are discussed with them prevents these meetings from disintegrating into sessions of frivolous backbiting and loveless criticism.

The Bishop is obliged by the laws of the Church to seek the advice, at least every ten years at the diocesan synod, of various representatives of the clergy concerning methods and goals to be followed and sought in the care of the souls in his diocese. Through the Bishop's authority the conclusions reached obtain the force of law. Besides these prescriptions of the law, Bishops have at all times on their own discussed their problems and methods with priests as well as laymen. There is, therefore, nothing new in the idea of lay and clerical dialogue.

Naturally the supreme authorities of a diocese or episcopal court cannot take counsel with their subjects before every single prescription they make. To demand that they do so would be contrary to good sense and the spirit of obedience. Moreover the trust and spirit of obedience which the subject ought to feel in the presence of his superior should not be changed by the fact that he may now advise him.

One who cares for his soul may occasionally, after
mature deliberation and humble prayer, arrive at the
conviction that a particular prescription of a higher
superior does not take into full account certain
concrete circumstances. In such a case the subject
should withhold all uncharitable criticism, become
conscious of his personal responsibility towards the
superior, enter into a more vital contact with him
and try to make it easier for him to have access to
reality and the needs of other men.

The relationship of the layman to his pastor should
be similar to that of the pastor to his Ordinary. It
may be that a vigilant, exceptional and religiously
formed layman will fly off the handle and affirm here
and now that his pastor has failed somewhere along
the line or is old-fashioned, or in a rut, etc. But in
final analysis who practices obedience best: the
thoughtless one who refuses to work along with the
pastor or the critical, discerning person who first
draws his own conclusions and then tries to influence
his pastor in a prudent way? Needless to say the
one who is deliberately uncharitable in his criticism
does not obey conscientiously nor is he a mature
Christian. Even responsible criticism must be offered in a prudent and charitable way. The father

of a family, for example, wants his child's baptism
to be as beautiful as one that he saw in a liturgically
conscious parish. He is adamant in his stand that the
baptism of his child will not take place in a corner.
But will he at the same time speak with others of
similar mind about what they can contribute to one
of the greatest gifts of God, a worthy baptism? If
so, he may speak to the pastor, but he should certainly not hit him on the head with a statement like,
"You're about as backward a pastor as I've ever come
across," but rather in accord with truth and love
he should approach him by saying, "Certainly you,
too, have often wished that baptism in our parish
could be emphasized more and that the newly bap-
tized should be touchingly received by the whole
parish as a new child of the great family of God.
We've also thought the matter over and would be
more than glad to cooperate."

b. Conscience and civil authority

All classic textbooks of Catholic moral theology
hold that, unless the contrary be proven, the presumption is for the validity of the commands and

laws of civil as well as spiritual authority. Does that
hold generally today also for civil authority? Basing
ourselves on the experiences of modern times with
men who lack faith and morals often elevated to
high positions in the State, we can no longer hold
the position that moral theologians formerly have
rightly demanded. In view of the 20th-century dic-
tatorships and totalitarian regimes known to us, who
can say any more that, "Until the contrary is proved
I trust that those in charge in my country are commanding justly?" Where is one to go to acquire
such trust? With the de-Christianization of politics
and the wide-spread presence of non- or even anti-
Christian regimes in the world, a much more critical
sense seems more in keeping with reality. One's
basic attitude towards every legitimate superior must,
however, remain the same, namely, a sincere readiness to obey coupled with a spirit of charity and
responsibility. Moreover, by reason of this spirit
of love and responsibility, one must continually ask
himself anew, "What is there here of true obedience?"

Blind obedience is never a Christian obedience.
God does not want blind obedience but intelligent
obedience, an obedience that sees all things in the
light of love. He does not want a forced obedience

but rather desires that obedience which flows from one's free will and personal evaluation of each concrete situation in which he is asked to obey.

Through his grace God fits the man to the task. St. Paul, St. Augustine and all the great theologians teach us that this is the essence of the law of the New Testament, that God demands from us only that which he has already given to us, and in his giving he reveals the wisdom of his will. We would indeed be guilty of extreme pride in placing our limited understanding above that of Almighty God by preparing ourselves to disobey him even after having clearly understood the reasons behind the things he commands. We are not much less guilty when we refuse to obey him without this clear understanding for our obedience to God is truly enlightened whenever we obey through faith. We must be fully convinced that when God demands something of us he has already given us the necessary graces to enable us to obey, and when he gives us some task to do he has already given us the strength we need to get it done. We need not examine each detail, although God does love to have us recognize ever more and more the glory of the wisdom behind his every command.

With human authority it is an entirely different matter. Especially in regard to godless possessors of authority we are bound to obey only after we have made a very earnest examination to determine whether their commands and laws are justified or not. We must then subject ourselves to civil authorities according to the words and spirit of St. Peter, "Be subject to every human creature for God's sake" (1 Peter 2, 13).

Because it is God's will we must be ready to obey civil authorities but we must also "prove the spirits" (1 John 4, 1). Only in those cases where authority has been established by God and legitimately commands do we stand before an actual prescription of God, and therefore only in those cases do the words of St. Paul hold: "He who resists such authority resists the ordinance of God" (Rom. 13, 2).

Conscientious obedience must again and again ask the question, "Does human authority command here in the name of God?" In this matter the following principles hold:

1. All just laws bind in conscience. This holds true also for toll and tax laws according to the words of St. Paul, "Wherefore you must needs be subject, not only because of the wrath, but also for con-

science sake. For this is also why you pay tribute; for they are the ministers of God, serving unto this very end. Render to all men whatever is their due: tribute to whom tribute is due, taxes to whom taxes are due" (Rom. 13, 5ff.). The obligation to conscientious obedience does not depend on whether the lawgiver expressly calls on our conscience or not. We are immediately bound in conscience by the justice of the law itself.

But for a law to be just it must be in some way necessary or useful for the common good. The fact that a law or a prescription does not directly or positively contradict a natural law does not yet make it a just law; for precisely the superfluity of unnecessary laws is something very burdensome to man's nature and is actually opposed to the efficient functioning of authority. Hence truly unnecessary laws are not to be called just simply because, by reason of their inner justice, they can bind one in conscience. For the sake of good order, in cases of doubt, the necessity of such laws and with that their justification is generally to be accepted.

2. Not only do laws that are absolutely impossible not oblige, but also those which cannot practically be fulfilled and those that are morally unbearable.

For it is equally unjust that human authorities demand too much from their subjects. When Christ
said of his law, "My yoke is easy and my burden
light" (Matt. 11, 30), he had no intention to subject
men to unsuitably hard or practically unbearable
human laws and commands. In case of great necessity, of course, extraordinary things can be demanded.
If an essential part of a law, which cannot be entirely
fulfilled, is just and possible, that part must be com-
plied with. If, for example, the entire amount of
taxes cannot possibly be paid, one must pay the
part that is considered just and that can be paid.

3. In regard to patently unjust laws one is certainly not bound, because the very reason for obliging
is no longer present, namely, the justice of the law.
But, and this is not to be overlooked, there are often
other circumstances that bring about another type
of obligation in conscience, presupposing that what
is commanded is not bad in itself (for what is evil
in itself as, for example, the killing of the mentally
ill, can never oblige even if it be commanded by
one's superior). When only the imposition of the
obligation on the part of human authority is unjust
but the thing commanded is not bad in itself, the
common good rightly understood or the relationship

it has with one's own good or that of others, can sometimes call for conscientious obedience, not by reason of the unjustly commanding superior, but in view of the good of society.

If we were to deny to authorities all that, according to our judgment, perhaps even according to a mature, impartial judgment, appeared unnecessary, we would often be passively resisting authority. There could result from this much disorder and irritation over the apparent disobedience of Christians. Flagrant disregard for laws that in themselves are not bad and can easily be obeyed would reasonably anger authority. Such conduct, further, could create more problems than it would solve for the person disobeying.

A father of a family could, for example, for various reasons be obliged to pay taxes which, according to his mature and deliberate judgment, clearly imply injustice. He sees that if he does not pay he will be punished as a tax-evader and he and his family might lose their citizenship, and perhaps even their daily bread. Hence, because his refusal to pay his unjust taxes might result in much greater disadvantages to himself and others, a well-ordered love of self, charity towards his neighbor, his consideration for the good name of the Church, etc., would oblige him to bear what the authorities have placed on him in an unjust manner.

The judgment that one is not bound by an unjust law presupposes a genuine relation to society, an impartial understanding of the common good, and a mature consideration of the situation. The affirmation alone that the demand of the superior is unjust does not allow us immediately to draw the conclusion that we need not in any way obey it.

4. We must obey rulers who are sinners just as we would obey those who are holy, in so far as they are legitimate bearers of authority and their commands or laws are not unjust. We must also, through genuine obedience, honor in them the authority established by God.

Not only the rules of good sportsmanship and fair-play, but Christian morality itself strictly forbids us to undermine authority because of the personal failings and sins of the rulers, which have nothing to do with their vocational suitability.

5. If the superior commands something that is not only unjust but even sinful in itself, we must deny him obedience in such things under all conditions for the sake of our conscience. We must at

least practice passive opposition in so far as we do not carry out the command. Oftentimes it will be necessary to speak out loudly in order to preserve others from sin and occasionally we will even have to instruct the superior himself for his own good.

When State officials go so far as to completely upset the harmony within the State itself and instead of caring for the common good, wish to introduce a licentious party egoism or try to force the people to sin in important matters, and in a certain sense in all things, responsible men must do all they can to stop these abuses and if necessary and possible, to overthrow the regime.

c. Conscientious obedience or absolute fidelity of the subject

A brief, historical, religious, sociological study should help us to understand more clearly the genuine concept of true Christian conscientious obedience. Among most pagans the question, "What must one do in view of sinful commands?" is hardly faced with clarity, let alone with Christian virtue. In German history the fidelity of the people to the

ruler has always been something absolute, something of the highest order. The subject never felt
the need to ask or to examine whether the job assigned was something good, whether the ruler called
him to a war of pillage or to a just one of self-defense.
The man simply had to preserve his fidelity without
any deliberation. For us Christians this immoral
idea of "absolute fidelity" to any man became through
the State-Church, to the Germanic peoples who had
gone over to Arianism, no essential remedy but
rather a kind of religious consecration. The religious
glamor that the State-Church authorities loaned to
the German princes seemed to the subject to forbid
any critical examination.

In Catholic Middle Ages the tension between the
Church and civil authorities, between papacy and
emperor, served as a protection against the subject's
exaggerated sense of fidelity opposing his spirit of
true conscientious obedience. The many points of
opposition between the two powers, especially the
Church's rebukes against the abuse of civil power,
enabled the subjects to form their own judgments
more easily. The late Middle-Age nominalism introduced a fatal relapse. The denial of an inviolable
essential law, the teaching that God does not com-

mand because the thing commanded is in itself good, but vice-versa, that the thing commanded is good only because the divine will (arbitrary will) desires it, made possible the glorification of the arbitrary will of civil rulers.

How the ancient and indestructible pagan idea of the subject's unconditional fidelity to his lord lived on in the depths of the soul is shown by the ease with which the German princes, at the time of the great religious wars, appropriated to themselves the *jus reformandi* (the right to prescribe a new religion for their subjects). The most frightening point in all this is that one did not seem to feel, either on the Catholic or on the Evangelical side, what monstrous offense against the truth of Christian liberty it was that the princes could prescribe over-night a new religion for their subjects. The Christian conscience should have cried out loudly. On the Catholic side a few did protest firmly when an heretical prince had forced his subjects into heresy; but it was something else again when Catholic princes energetically led back to the house of truth and grace those who had been torn away from the Church by force. It remains a great scandal that the princes of any era could decide concerning the religion of their subjects, but especially that this could happen after a thousand years of Christianity. Had not the Church from the very beginning taught that no one can be forced to embrace the true faith?

In this regard the new State-Church, coming with Protestantism, had frightening results. Not only did the State-independent Church court fall as a blockade against the arbitrariness of princes, but also the position of conscience itself, in regard to State-Church authority, was shaken, since Lutheran teaching discarded the concept of any absolute validity in the divine prescriptions contained in the Gospel. The ordinances of creation are, according to the teaching of Luther, more or less annihilated by original sin, or at least have become unknowable. The conscience of men is nothing more than a burnt out ruins. Thus one understands that the Christian does not dare to examine critically the commands of the princes who ruled "by divine power" or to deny obedience to him. The solution of the reformers was this: In all cases adjust yourself to the necessary ordinances of a sinful world, just as it is, so that it will at least make room for you as an individual when you want to seek God in personal intimacy. Along the same line lay the Lutheran grasp of life

which culminates in the admonition to resign oneself and be content with the situation as it stands.

According to Lutheran teaching the Gospel gives
a norm for the instruction of princes, but doesn't,
any more than the natural moral law, give any one
the right to have recourse to his own conscience and
deny obedience to a command of civil authority.
Added to this was an over-emphasis on the "civil
function of the law" on the part of Lutheran preachers
who saw in civil law a protection against the logical
consequences of their teaching that the Gospel gives
no juridical orders.

Thus the teaching of the reformers, which today
is freely discussed also by Protestant theologians,
together with old German ideals, and those of the
nominalists of the late Middle Ages, are to a great
extent responsible that the German people—the in-
fection includes also the Catholics and to some extent other nationalities—became an extremely subservient people.   The terrors of national socialism
have brought about an awakening.   But many, who
in their unlimited subjection, became guilty of the
greatest crimes, even after the war excused themselves
by saying, "A command is a command.   I was ordered

to do it. It was not for me to ask whether it was good or evil."

In the face of this situation we Catholics have every reason to educate our members, also in regard to Church authority, to genuine maturity, to an ever more charitable but not less vigilant distinction and responsibility, in order that they may become truly mature also in regard to the influence of modern mass psychology and the propaganda of certain totalitarian States, as well as in regard to the "beast out of the deep" which threatens us. If we do not educate men first in the field of Church life to a mature capability of discerning right from wrong, to a vigilant sense of responsibility, to a conscientious obedience in the Holy Spirit, they will never find the courage to publicly profess their convictions regarding the nature and limits of civil authority and the undesirability of any totalitarian State. The Catholic who is well instructed in his faith, and steadfast in his spirit of true and faithful obedience to the Church, will be the last one ever to be tempted to join any totalitarian anti-God regime.

III

Community-Forming Love and
the Personal Power of Love

*"We are children of the freewoman
in virtue of the freedom
wherewith Christ has made us free."*
(Gal. 4, 31)

COMMUNITY-FORMING LOVE AND THE PERSONAL POWER OF LOVE

OBEDIENCE, REVERENCE AND LOVE

The relationship of Christians to authority is not exhausted in the mere ideas of "command and obey." The soul of the genuine exercise of authority and obedience is love. The conscientious obedience which superiors and subjects offer Almighty God, and their common responsibility for the community, have their proper source in love and in the love-filled liberty of the children of God along with the lively appreciation of values nourished by it. Love shows itself above all in reverence for one another, in a loving reverence which sees the mystery of God behind all things and in all things. It has a presentiment, at least darkly, of God's plan which proceeds from love and never debases a fellow man to the status of a mere instrument.

Holy Scripture emphasizes reverence as an essential component of obedience, especially in the family. Children owe their parents reverence above all else. Without it their obedience would be very imperfect. Parents, on the other hand, in exercising their rights as superiors, must especially honor the child of God in their son or daughter. When St. Paul insists on the obligation of a wife to obey her husband, he gives this obedience, because of the reverence which it should comport, a new beauty: "Let each one of you also love his wife just as he loves himself; and let the wife respect the husband" (Eph. 5, 33). The reverence must be mutual: "Men should honor their wives as co-heirs of grace and life" (1 Peter 3, 7). Reverence has its root in the knowledge of the depth of the mysteries in which they have dignity from God. When the wife, out of reverence for the great mystery of love between Christ and the Church, obeys in her husband the same Christ (Eph. 5, 23) who earned the loving obedience of his bride, our holy mother the Church, through the complete giving of himself in love, then she experiences her obedience not as something worthy of men but rather as being worthy of God. Mere subjection to a man because he is physically

and socially stronger than she would not be worthy
of the Christian wife; it would not be an expression
of the liberty that is hers as a child of God nor would
it correspond to her love for Christ.   And the husband should not presume on his strength or ego-
tistically make use of his social advantage.   He must
gain her reverence in so far as he loves her "as Christ
loved the Church and delivered himself up for it"
(Eph. 5, 25).   The Christian man, whose authority
recalls the authority of Christ, must in reverence
know that the Christian woman symbolizes the holy
mystery of the Church as "bride of the Lamb."   In
Christian marriage the preeminence of authority
obliges him to a special service of love and the wife
to genuine obedience in a spirit of love for the sacra-
ment gives a special dignity and power to the heart
of each.   This tender mystery is disturbed when
men (by having recourse to Holy Scripture) and
women (by having recourse to civil law) seek to
rule the household independently of one another.

What holds in Christian marriage concerning
the obedience of love, which can come only from
true reverence, and concerning authority which gives
a basis for the excellence of unselfish, reverential,
self-sacrificing service, must also distinguish our

relationship with Church authority. We should see in the Church not her external ruling power but her self-sacrificing pastoral care. The deepest mystery of the Church should be always present to us, namely, that it is the bride of the Lamb, the beloved of the Son of the Father. To her the Lord has entrusted the mystery of His heart; and to her has he given, as the precious bond of his love, the Holy Spirit. The Church deserves not just any kind of obedience, it merits first love and then the obedience that flows spontaneously from this love.

OBEDIENCE UNDER THE LAW OF THE CROSS

We love and obey the Church as it is, not merely as it will be when it appears on the great day of the Lord as the new Jerusalem, "without spot or wrinkle." With faith in the crucified love of Christ for his Church we persevere amid the tensions of this life. Our obedience must take its meaning from the law of the cross. Christ has merited the gift of the Church for himself through his obedience on the cross. He suffered *for* the Church—and what was perhaps even more difficult—He suffered *in* his Church, not only in Judas but also in Peter, and in all who in the beginning fought, but in the hour of trial took to flight. During his passion he had before his eyes all the sins that would be committed in his Church and through it. So we must not wonder if we have to suffer sometimes for the Church. Nor is it something to brag about from the rooftops. Ours must rather be a quiet, reverent, and in essence, an ever trustful suffering. Christ redeemed the world by means of an obedience that was painful because it led him to death out of love. We must not fly from obedience when it starts to be painful, whether it be that it goes against our self-love or our laziness, or whether it be that we want for ourselves a more perfect command. In so far as we take upon ourselves the cross of obedience to earthly authority in a spirit of faith and love, our obedience shares in the glory of the Redeemer's love in as much as a ray of the glory of our heavenly King has fallen on all legitimate authority. As long as the imperfection of this world lasts, our relationship to authority, especially to civil authority, but also to Church authority, will always be accompanied by difficulties which elevate only him whom love preserves.

We believe in the Church, in its final state of perfection and in its sublime mystery in Christ Jesus. We believe in her even when we ourselves, through imperfect or even bad obedience, and others, perhaps on account of our defective or bad commanding, obscure this mystery in the sight of the unbelieving world.   Out of this faithful, reverential love comes the courage to call the attention of the superiors, when it is the time and place, to failings and mistakes, whether it be in secret or in public just as St. Paul "withstood to his face" the first Pope, his beloved brother (Gal. 2, 14).   It is consonant with childlike love for the Church that we not only struggle on our part for an ever more perfect obedience, but that we strive with our superiors for a better issuing of commands.   The thought that even the unlettered Christian must sometimes help his superiors in this way and according to the measure of his gifts and capabilities is not a fashionable idea in our democratic age, although it appears especially apt today.   The old Canon Law took from a compendium of theology an impressive passage "*de peccato taciturnitatis*" which condemns "the sins of subjects who without love or through cowardice are silent concerning the faults and mistakes of their superiors." The superiors, who are also mere men, need the vigilance and mature discerning love of their subjects, in order that they might fulfill their office for God's honor and that they themselves might become ever more Christ-like. Uncharitable criticism and even more, hypocritic flattery, can only ruin a superior, weaken his authority, and finally destroy the spirit of the community. As the superior must know that he has been placed through love in the service of the community and of each subject, so the subject, in a spirit of genuine Christian obedience, must help the superior to be a better representative of God's authority. He can do this through his love, kindness, personal well-wishing, prayer, and also, in case of necessity, by talking things over with his superior and warning him.

VICTORY OVER COLLECTIVISM THROUGH LOVE

The great danger of today lies in collectivism, the spirit of the masses and the spirit of the collective authority borne by it which seeks only a submissive following. All of us, not excepting those in authority, stand in danger of mass organization. To this, the practice of Church and civil authority and the art of practicing obedience may give no support. In the first place, a genuinely human contact between the one who commands and the one who obeys, a relationship of trust, love and mutual reverence, is necessary. It is not enough to honor the office of the superior. We must meet him with a love that is not hypocritical in order that we do not end by seeing in him merely an impersonal instrument for the maintaining of order. It does not cost us much personally to recognize an abstract authority. More difficult than a YES to the office is a charitable and well-wishing YES to *this* legitimate possessor of authority, a YES to our own personal responsibility for him and his task. That would make his job easier and our obedience more praise-worthy. The nature of Christian obedience implies more than mere subjection; it includes solidarity and loving responsiblity for the community, its superior and each individual member. When the relationship of superior to subject is animated with a joint, fervent love for the community, there will not so easily be Church bureaucrats in high offices.

Do not we, the subjects and also the superiors,

need to make an earnest examination of conscience when an impassionate sociologist like Max Weber writes: "The purest kind of the "legal type" of power is the bureaucratic government. The relationships within the modern state, among its commerce officials, among the priestly ranks in the modern Catholic hierarchy, between officials and employees of our banks and the heads of capitalistic industries represent the most important examples of just such a power structure." (*Gesammelte Aufsätze zur Religions-soziologie*, Tübingen, 1922, I, S. 272.) The qualification of modern Catholic priests by Max Weber is doubtless too succint; taken as a general rule it tends to deny them proper reverence. In order that we may be able to reject it as unfitting, we, the subjects, must make greater effort not to degrade those commanding by our spiritless obedience, and our uncharitable criticism. Who does not see that a relationship to them, understood in purely juridical terms, must at once conjure up ghosts of medieval Church bureaucrats?

Superiors must examine themselves again and again to see if they merely apply dead paragraphs of the law or, as is their honorable privilege (if they are in the least concerned for their subjects), if they truly respect the dignity of the community and of each individual in it entrusted to their care, and, finally, if they open up men's hearts to the love of God. This is possible for them on a permanent basis only if their subjects can meet them in a personal relationship of trust, well-wishing, warm Christian love and community-minded responsibility.

If we once effect a personal relationship between superiors and subjects in Church circles, according to the laws of psychology and sociology, the relationship between civil authorities and citizens, yes even between the directors of commerce and their employees, must make essential gains in becoming more human.

We acquire a correct relationship to authority first of all through a loving, trusting relationship of obedience to God, from whom all human power is derived. But the opposite can at times prove to be equally true for wherever one's relationship to authority is realized in a mutual spirit of love and reverence, a soul-experience is given to him that makes it easier for him to find the right relationship of reverence and of loving obedience to God. If we open our own hearts to the love of God and give others access to it as well, we will have achieved

more than external success. The Son of God, in his
incarnation, passion and death, has taught us to
despise quick, external, man-organized success. His
final victory through the resurrection awakens in us
a trust in our personal victory which we must buy
at the price of humble obedience and serving, unselfish love.

IV

Religious Liberty

"The truth shall make you free."
(John 8, 32)

RELIGIOUS LIBERTY

THE CHURCH AND LIBERTY

The Church and Liberty is one of the subjects that called for much attention in the second Vatican Council and in world public opinion, and which characterizes in a particular way the new situation in which the Church has met the changes which the modern world has undergone. In just what does the problem consist? Is it simply a question of a diplomatic adaptation to a world in which the Church can no longer impose its own authority with force, through which, where Catholics are in the minority, it appeals to liberty of conscience, while where they are in the majority it invokes respect for the sincere convictions of each one's conscience? The well-known theory of the "thesis of truth" and the "hypothesis of tolerance in case of necessity" seemed to move in this direction. But now the time has come to make a clean sweep of such a scale of values composed of two weights and two measures in order that the Church may preach and give testimony to the Gospel in a credible manner. In order to understand —not to justify—the judgments and the practices of the Church in the past we must take into account the historical and social conditions of those times of intolerance. Today there is a question not only of simple adaptation to changed circumstances, but we are witnessing a precious and significant development that finds its justification in the Gospel itself. However, before confronting the problem of religious liberty (about which the Council has already amply spoken), it is necessary to clarify the very idea of liberty.

When we speak of Christian liberty we think above all of the liberty of Christ, and secondly of that liberty by which Christ has made us free. The resurrection is the great sign of the liberty that has triumphed in humility and in meekness without any use of violence or restriction. The measure that is placed before our eyes is the full participation in Christ's liberty and the way to attain it is his way of humility, meekness and love that does no violence to another man's liberty.

LIBERTY IN ITS BEGINNING

We shall share fully in the liberty of Christ only when in heaven, in an eternal communion of love, we contemplate God face-to-face. Here below our liberty is still in a state of development, ever increasing and ever threatened. For us on earth it is not only a gift already given but one for which we must constantly strive. Here below we can never consider it as a good that is already absolutely secure. We can, however, preserve it if we receive with gratitude that portion of it which has been destined for us. However, we must always remember that the liberty of each individual is connected with the liberty of others. The individualism of the last century ascribed to each one a perfect, almost divine liberty.

Similar erroneous opinions are found in some moralists who affirm that it is morally possible for every man, at every moment to perform any task whatsoever. It is sufficient that he have a good will in order to go ahead and act. The long tradition of the Church, however, and the progress of present day psychology give us a sounder doctrine. Man

possesses a liberty that is conditioned by psychological heredity, by his surroundings, and especially by
his opportunities. Only the man who, conscious of
his responsibility in his dealings with others, strives
to create a spirit of liberty in the family and in
the other social structures, can have a well-founded
hope of enjoying a higher and nobler degree of
liberty in his daily life. The individualist, on the
other hand, who would like to preserve only his
own liberty and that of his family and friends, will
eventually grow melancholy, become a slave of his
own egoism, and in the end, of his environment.
The man, however, who lives in union with Christ,
who bears the burdens of his neighbor, will, because
of this, become a sharer in an ever greater liberty.

NATURAL MORAL LIBERTY

When we speak of Christian liberty we must
distinguish between purely moral and natural *freedom,* given to every man with his nature, and the
holy *liberty* of the children of God. Moral liberty,
which consists in the power and in the capacity to
choose the good, is essential in any discussion of

religious liberty. When one affirms that liberty consists in the power of choosing indifferently good or evil, he is on a dangerous path. The liberty of God does not include the power to choose evil, but only the power to do good. Man is morally free when he is in a condition to choose the good in so far as it is good. The degree of such liberty depends on the degree of one's moral conscience. Liberty signifies at least that one is conscious of an obligation inherent in each and every person to do the good. This, however, is only a lower degree of one's moral conscience. Authentic human liberty aspires to a knowledge of values.

Of course a father and mother cannot always indicate to a child precisely in what true values consist. Nevertheless the child must trust its parents. In the course of a normal education the child is taught to discover the WHY of things, that is, the values, the enticing satisfaction behind fulfillment of one's duty and the splendor found in moral goodness. Such knowledge becomes more and more attractive and enlightening as one matures. It proceeds intuitively as the natural expression of a being permeated with love. When a man fulfills his duty, when he becomes better, and when he experiences goodness also in others, he acquires an ever deeper knowledge of the good. The highest degree of moral knowledge consists in seeing all things in the fountain of pure love which comes from God; in this regard not only do we know that God is good but also that all his precepts are a manifestation of his goodness.

CHRISTIAN LIBERTY

Christian liberty, as the holy liberty of the children of God, is something more. It consists in an intimate relationship with the spirit of Christ, or, as St. Paul says (Rom. 8), it is the "law of the spirit which gives us life in Christ Jesus and has freed us from the law of sin." It is the law of the Spirit which gives us life; that is, a law written in the heart, not a law imposed from without. It is a sharing in the joy of God. The primary characteristic of the liberty of God's children is the ability to recognize it as God's own gift. God manifests himself to us especially through his gifts, his goodness, his love, his truth. Therefore, our response must always be an answer of gratitude, joy and love. Here below we are always striving towards the holy liberty of the children of God. We do not possess it yet in a perfect measure. Therefore we need to exercise it in a two-fold way. We cannot be content with a theoretical education in obedience. Our education in it must also be a practical introduction to the liberty of the children of God. A morality is not Christian because it concentrates its attention primarily on exterior ordinances, on commands and precepts imposed from without. That which designates it as typically Christian is not the distinction that it makes between mortal and venial sins. We do not see the true face of the Church when we see it through the lens of Canon Law. The Church educates us to the holy liberty of the children of God through the Gospel, the joyful good news.

CANON LAW TAKES SECOND PLACE

Canon Law has a protective function, but of a secondary nature. St. Thomas affirms this repeatedly, both in the *Summa Theologica* and still more in his *Commentaries on the Letters of St. Paul.* He says in several places that the primary element of the

New Law is the grace of the Holy Spirit. Therefore in Christian education the gifts of the Holy Spirit are a fundamental starting point. That education errs which does nothing but give commands: "Do this; do not do that!" A child thus educated will never gain any naturalness and spontaneity in carrying out the wishes of his parents. Nor will he succeed in perceiving real moral values. St. Bernard, in his *Liber de Consolatione* to Pope Eugene regarding a danger that threatened the Church in that epoch, complains in these words, "Throughout the whole day laws make a great deal of noise in your palace. And what laws? Those of Justinian, not of the Lord." Then he proposes as a remedy the right order of things: "First meditation on the divine word; secondly, preaching of the Gospel; and finally, also laws." The first thing that guarantees true liberty, that is, the liberty of doing good and doing it joyfully and intelligently, is meditation on the divine word and on the love of God. In the second place, our liberty is guaranteed only when the Church places its trust in the joyful proclamation of this holy liberty of the children of God. Its annunciation is a joyful message that awakens in us an enthusiasm for doing good. And here the words of the priest, Esdras, in the book of Nehemias are applicable: "Go ... take a part of the feast to those who could not come. The joy of the Lord is indeed our strength."

THE ADDRESS OF POPE JOHN IN THE COUNCIL

The problem of religious liberty which faced the Council must be understood from Pope John's point of view. It is not right to react to the mistakes of erring men by pure and simple condemnation. It is much more important to discover their aspirations to the good and to see in them, according to the will of God, his children. We must begin by announcing to them the joyful good news of the Gospel for this is the pedagogy that our Lord has taught us. Did he not, at the culminating moment of his prophetic mission in the room of the Last Supper, proclaim a New Law: "Love one another as I have loved you," and then quickly add: "I no longer call you servants because the servant does not know what the Master does. Rather I call you friends because all that I have heard from my Father

I have revealed to you?" From this it evidently follows that only a joyful and positive annunciation of the Gospel which takes into account the aspirations of modern man and of the peoples of today, can reawaken the true spirit of the liberty of the friends of Christ. Man must know that he will not be able to associate himself with this intimate knowledge of liberty if at the same time he does not allow himself to be changed internally according to the example of the goodness of Christ.

To give liberty to men signifies also to admit them to the free choice of acceptation or repudiation of the Gospel. Such choice is a risk. When a man, notwithstanding everything, chooses evil, there will be the truth and the Gospel itself to accuse him of his error. "The Spirit will convince the world of its error." Men animated by the Holy Spirit do not live under the restrictions of a law imposed from without, but they live in the joy and in the deep conviction of being witnesses of the truth. It is their behavior that will convince the world of its error.

It is a risk to grant religious liberty. However, God did not hesitate to take it. He wished to have friends, not slaves, and friendship necessarily presupposes the possibility of choice. For this reason he has granted it, looking of course to the example of love and goodness that Christ has already given us.

Our task is to render the goodness and truth of God visible, not only in abstract concepts, in philosophical formulas, in theological outlines, or in the sepulchral tones of a dead language, but in a living dialogue with all men, being ready to discover traces of truth in all races, creeds and nationalities.

In fact, what is there of vitality in human life if one's free choice of religion is impeded? Absolutely nothing, since the man who already lies in the tomb can no longer lose his life. There is a natural and universal tendency in man to preserve orthodoxy of faith by means of a dead language and dead formulas. In reality, when this is done, nothing is risked or preserved since truth has already departed from time. It is indeed either a salutary life-giving truth, the truth of Christ, or it is not truth at all because it is no longer vital. This risk in choosing is a perfectly normal one because it pertains to the natural risks of any life in the process of development. In our so-called Christian society, on the other hand, liberty has often been wanting, and the case of Galileo is only a typical example. In it there was an absence of that joy and trust which is born of a living faith. The supporters and the representatives of the Inquisition lacked in many respects an intuitive knowledge of the truth, a knowledge that is born of faith and connatural to it.

NOT A MONOPOLISTIC SOCIETY

A closed mind is social in origin, the result of a closed society's battle against the attacks of other closed societies. Some centuries after the Constantinian era a kind of monopolistic Christian society was formed. To many it seemed that the Church had a right, based on a monopoly not only on revealed truth but on culture in general, to control everything. Generally the clergy kept this monopoly in their own hands. Present-day studies concerning the psychological structure of the monopolistic society indicate that whereas a society in which freedom of competition reigns must gain the sympathy of public opinion, the monopolistic society need not do so. This fact alone, however, has very serious repercussions in the very heart of the monopolistic society itself. One of these can be seen for example in the polemic, if not very edifying, intrigues and conflicts among various schools of theology and, to be quite frank, even among religious orders which is the same as saying even among brothers. All this in-fighting is simply the logical end product of a closed society in the process of transforming itself into a monopolistic one. Yet neither the Gospel nor the Church itself was ultimately responsible for this state of affairs. Only social reality can be held to blame.

Today we live in a pluralistic society in which many different ethical systems face us. In order to meet competition they present themselves in their most attractive form, accenting the advantages that they have to offer. What a pity it would be if the Church in our time did not, with all the resources she has at her command, succeed in presenting the Gospel, the joyful good news of Christ, in an appealing way. The Church is conscious of its election and of its particular and unique mission, but it cannot claim to possess a monopoly on truth. To do this would be to oppose the Gospel itself. In the first joyful message we read: "In the beginning God created man to his image," and "the heavens show forth the wonders of the Lord to all men."

Man has preserved a part of this truth and sometimes the members of other religions and other
Christian communities have developed some aspect
of our common inheritance well, and frankly, better
than the true Church, the Catholic Church, has done.
Certainly the abolition of slavery was a consequence
and a fruit of Christianity. However, oftentimes
there have been non-Catholics who have brought
forth more valid arguments and opposed slavery
with more vigor than Catholics. To admit this
simply means to adore the Holy Spirit, who breathes
where he wills. A good part of religious liberty consists in recognizing the good present in others as
a gift of God. Only by so doing will we become
truly capable of accepting a pluralistic society in
which we must collaborate with all for the good of
all men in so far as they have something which is
of positive value to present.

TRUTH IS ALWAYS PERSONAL

A second aspect of religious liberty is of a more
human and personal character. Intolerance does not

immediately concern itself with the individual. It follows, instead, an abstract truth and often thinks it can define it without involving others and keep it pure without a deep and intimate adaptation to them in love. From this, too, rises the temptation to present theology solely in the terms of a dead language. Certainly a formulated truth exists in an abstract manner as well. But divine truth is a salutary truth. The word of God in the Bible is always bound to actuality; it is always formulated for the service of the salvation of *this* people and of *this* determined culture. For that reason it would be absurd and a mistake to be content to read the Bible to the man of today in Latin or Hebrew. The Church has the task of translating the joyful message of the Gospel into the language of everyday life and to make it something actual to those living today. It must constantly learn how to adapt to the times from the inspired pages of scripture themselves, and then it must proclaim God's message on the wave lengths of modern life.

Truth in this world has always been entrusted to certain persons. It made its incarnate appearance in the person of Jesus Christ. Christ is the truth in person and he does not present the truth in abstract formulas. Certainly he announced a truth valid for all centuries, but he preached it to fishermen and to the humble people by whom he was surrounded in a way that touched their heart. Thus he introduced into the world a division of spirits. The problem is that of a formulation of the truth commensurate with men in flesh and blood who are still searching for perfect truth. We Catholics, however, do not possess all the truth. The Church is not in a position to offer to the world of today ready and timeless solutions for the actual problems which were formerly unknown. It must recognize that in regard to infallible decisions, which do not mature every day, there exists also the possibility of assuming a position in which it decides to examine a determined problem meanwhile simply indicating the direction in which the solution is to be sought.

The defenders of religious liberty know that under normal conditions religious knowledge is something that makes progress gradually. They know, too, that it advances much more quickly if the faith is presented joyfully and if accent is placed more decisively on the liberating force of truth. This truth, as Pope John often said, is of itself attractive. The holy liberty of the children of God can be preached only from testimony filled with a joyous faith, and cannot be imposed by force for then it would automatically be lost. When the joyful message of the Gospel is no longer apparent in Christianity a veil is drawn before the beatifying countenance of Almighty God. What is imposed is never or seldom loved. I know of many persons who are moral through blind faith alone and who do not love their state. The reason is because both father and mother were "moralists" and coldly imposed on them the precepts of the law. They were obliged to attend Church daily and to confess their sins once a month. In the scholastic age, too, people lived under a system of rigid surveillance and restriction. However, the reaction against these methods was not actually a reaction against the Gospel because they never learned to know the Gospel as the joyful good news that it really is. The love of God is attractive only for his friends. Therefore we must create an atmosphere of liberty and at the same time announce and bear wtiness through our example to

the joyful news of the Gospel. Only then can we
have trust in a love that attracts and in a truth that
has something to say to all men.

FAITH MAKES CONQUESTS IN LIBERTY

Certainly it is a risk. We must not forget that
religious liberty is threatened not only by the im-
perfections of its followers, but often and habitually
even more so by the indifferentism and dictates of
the world. It is threatened by evil which tries to
impose itself and therefore we must be prudent in
explaining what it really means. Good and evil do
not enjoy equal rights. Evil has no rights. Let us
take the case of a man in error. It can be that he
relies on his good conscience. However, he has
not made any effort to form his conscience, and now
he wishes to impose his opinion on others. In this
case the Church has the obligation to defend the
weak against the attempt of perversion through an
intolerable error. In so doing it is not difficult to
believe in the ultimate victory of truth and true
liberty provided that men can be placed in con-
frontation with evil and with error in a climate that

guarantees the free exercise of their God-given liberty
and, on the other hand, on condition that truth is
presented to them accompanied by that love which
keeps in mind the person addressed.

There are two conditions required of Christian
testimony. The world renovated by Christ is a
world subjected to ever new social upheavals which
necessitate new formulations of divine truth. In
the second place, there is a substantial difference
between the *freedom* of inert indifferentism and
the *liberty* that seeks to follow the truth.

It is in this context that we must approach the
pronouncement of the second Vatican Council regarding religious liberty and its condemnation of
indifferentism. In every case the more effacious
condemnation is that which presents religious liberty
and the faith in a positive light.

Religious liberty is threatened by the pessimism
of many Catholics. Pope Paul VI was right in his
marvelous discourse to the Italian episcopacy urging
them to free themselves from the shakles of the
negative aspects of reality with its risks and its
dangers, and to learn how to contemplate the marvelous action of God and the positive possibilities
for salvation prepared by him. When something the

Council proclaims does not agree with us, we too often have a tendency to become discouraged and to lose sight of the great lessons that God is giving us through it. Pessimism does not create an atmosphere in which a truth that is attractive and genuinely religious can long survive.

CONCLUSION

I close with homage to the memory of St. Francis. If in those times all Christians had adopted his methods and had had his heart and if they had presented themselves with one mind to the Sultans and his followers who were in error, that is, armed only with the arms of love, would not perhaps the Sultans have been converted to the truth? We cannot fight a good fight with crusades, terror and pessimism. They act very differently who liberate themselves from themselves as did the Saint of Assisi. Catholics who do not seek special privileges, who do not abuse the faith in order to create better social conditions for themselves, who remain faithful, too, when the faith costs them something, who free themselves from inborn egoism, who are a glorious testimony decisively lined up in favor of the light, these are the ones who create the conditions of true liberty for all those who are courageously searching for truth and love.